Canst thou draw out leviathan with an hook?

About the author

Jackie Wills was born in 1955 and won acclaim for her first collection, *Powder Tower,* which was a Poetry Book Society Recommendation and was shortlisted for the 1995 T. S. Eliot Prize. A journalist and editor of many years' experience, she has tutored creative writing workshops and read her own poetry at festivals and colleges around England. The recipient of several awards, among them writers' bursaries from South East Arts and the Arts Council of England, she has also held residencies on the Poetry Society Poetry Places scheme in the year 1999–2000, with Unilever Fabric Conditioners Category and elsewhere. She lives in Brighton with her partner and two children.

By the same author

Powder Tower (Arc, 1995)

PARTY

JACKIE WILLS

LEVIATHAN
OXFORD · PORTLAND · AMSTERDAM

First published in Great Britain in 2000 by
Leviathan
Market House
Market Place
Deddington
Oxford OX15 0SE

A CIP record for this book is available from the British Library

ISBN 1-903563-03-8 (cased)
1-903563-04-6 (paperback)

Editorial Director
Michael Hulse

Editorial Advisers
John Kinsella, Anne Michaels, Vincent O'Sullivan

Design
Claire Brodmann

Typesetting
Jeff Hames

Sales and Marketing
Drake International Services, Deddington, Oxford OX15 0SE

Distribution
BDL, Learoyd Road, Mountfield Industrial Estate, New Romney TN28 8XU

Printing and Binding
T. J. International Ltd., Padstow, Cornwall PL28 8RW

Contents

For my family

Author's acknowledgements

Acknowledgements are due to the editors of the following:

Wide Skirt, Stand, Outside Left (Ha'penny Press), *Independent, Poetry Review, The Real McCoy* (Out of the West).

'The North Downs Way' was commissioned by Kent County Council. The sequence of poems, 'Flight Paths', was written as a result of a Poetry Society/Countryside Agency Poetry Places residency from April to October 1999. 'Drought' was commissioned by Lever Brothers and Elida Fabergé during a residency from April to October 2000. Some of the poems in the 'Flight Paths' sequence were featured on BBC Radio 4 in 'Open Country'.

With great thanks to the Arts Council of England for a writing bursary in 1999 and to the K. Blundell Trust/Author's Foundation for a writing bursary in1997.

Publisher's acknowledgement

Leviathan wishes to thank Lever Brothers and Elida Fabergé for their generous assistance with procuring the cover art for this publication.

THE WOMAN WHO NEVER CALLED TIME

Regatta

The frigate moored in the harbour, F94 on its side,
raises its washing line of flags. This estuary,
separating two villages, could be a front line.
But the hillside houses are intact. Their occupants
welcome HMS *Brave* to the regatta, to protect
RAF jets which will fly stunts tonight, trail national colours,
shake yacht masts, rattle windows as they race
down the river and peel out of their tight diamond in arcs.
I've grown up with shows of force; recruiting tents
for army and navy at every county show.
Each year, a parade of fire-power
on Aldershot sports ground was made musical
with marching bands, every local common was littered
with spent shells. As children we knew red flags
meant firing on the ranges. We collected ration tins,
heated up single portions of sponge cake and custard,
sausages and beans. Trench food was stacked
in our larder with peaches and tomato soup.
Aldershot was our staging post, between home
and school. We learned which pubs to avoid
before a tour of duty. From the tops of buses,
we watched squaddies drill and at night,
in the precinct, MPs' jeeps rounding up the stopouts.

Brave hides her Exocets and Tomahawks below.
Her matt grey sides, invisible against the Falklands sea,
look like painted cardboard. We're fascinated by her,
the 270 men and women aboard in perfect uniforms,
fit for battle. Still, solid, self-contained,
she's like a mother to boats rippling water around her,
with such pleasure. We trust her not to aim guns
at children filling buckets with crabs. Like the jets,

MPs, drilling soldiers, we hope she'll never turn on us –
which is why we welcome her, invite crew
into the rowing race, explore her decks,
and join up. We want our children, fathers, brothers,
sisters, facing us with guns, to know us.

Rigging

If we'd taped that rainy night in the car
when we sat drinking with the windows down,
staring at the lights of two cottages
on the island opposite, it would play back
nothing but breathing, the door opening
and closing as you checked the children
in the tent, a cork pulled from a bottle,
the Atlantic below, reclaiming another inch
of the peninsula, wind rustling a plastic
rubbish bag, damp matches scraped uselessly
on the dashboard and you tapping a rhythm
on your glass with a pencil – like rigging
against masts, beached above the tideline,
bared of sails and wet with spray.

Diver

For nights after we call it off, rain heavy with pebbles
rattles the cracked glass of my windows, frame
knocking against frame, opening just enough
to release waves of draughts. My breath
is the only warmth in the room. Next door the dog howls
for absent owners. She'll wake the children,
their frightened heavy steps shaking
the boards. Rain drops from a broken gutter
like a water clock pushing a whittled float
slowly upwards to show the hours.
I'm down for 90 minutes, the deck steeper
than a river bank, in my steel suit
with joints of ball-bearings and rubber
moving like lids over eyes. I carry guncotton
to blast doors but the strong room opens
with hammer and chisel. I haul
a box of bullion through the wreck's weedy passages,
follow the rope back and count white stars
(the liner's mark) like chalk scrawled on trees
in dense pine woods, where there's no sky or grass
until the fire-break and you squint at the sun
wondering how long you've been following the trail.

Horses

You'd just left when the first explosion came
overhead, seconds between the light and blast.
I imagined the car lifted off the road, overturned
in a crater. At school I heard a thud one afternoon
– a bomb in the barracks, four miles away.
This storm, during the marching season,
could be happening over a November sea
at the start of it all. Four thousand horses
on transport ships searching for an anchorage
while stable boys below deck check tethers,
dodge hard heads and sing, the way I comfort
my daughter now. Then, a change in the wind
from east to west and a navigable bay.
Swimming ashore, the boys' fingers are plaited
into manes, as breakers lift them
off the horses' slippery backs
until hooves find purchase on the sand.
Above the beach, the village watches horses stagger
on ground that no longer rocks, sealed boxes
of ammunition piling up, as an army forms.

The Coastguard's Cottage

(*after Montale*)

You are watching the couple
with nothing to say to their child. I ask

if you remember being here
two months after our son was born.

Above us the coastguard's cottage moves:
plaster cracks, a skirting board gapes.

On the walls are experiments
with colour, squares of indigo, terracotta.

I could live there. You warn each storm
weakens the cliff a little more.

And my question's forgotten.
Perhaps I was alone feeding

him in the shade of an umbrella.
Have I replayed it wrong or too often?

Charts

Last night lightning flashed
inside the house, seeming to cut through
its granite walls. When I arrived
there was no power, just a room full of candles
and empty oyster shells from the coast
where Mont St Michel emerges from rock
and parties of walkers are led towards it
by a guide who knows the quicksands
and the tides. On the empty beach
I watch him burn to a silhouette, his small
party trusting him not to be wrong
about the time it will take them,
about the sea so far away you can only hear
it. After this walk, when everything except the mount
and dark line of trees they have left behind
is too far away to matter, they belong
with the monks pacing the cloisters.

Racecourse

I don't bet on horses, study tips
but I'd never put money on number six
side-stepping down the practice straight
turning circles at the starting gate.
A lark bursts out of scrub, so near
the horse flings himself into a rear
as if that southerly wind gave him wings
and amplified the scream that brings
all of us, sometime, to the edge of water
wishing it was solid enough to gallop over.

The Woman who never Called Time

He could still feel his finger after it was wrenched off.
I told him, "It's been burned. Gone up the hospital
chimney, with its bloody bandages, the pussed dressings,
placentae and limbs." But it felt the cold. Its ghost
stroked my back, up to the nape, tested for jags
on a surface he'd planed. Perhaps he should have buried
it in the garden. So we took on the pub. The Stag at Rest.
I never wanted to be a confessor or sneak. I met people
I wouldn't choose as friends, but learned to recognise
the crucial moments in darts and dominoes. Held my breath
with them. I watched men disappear, fingering a woman's sleeve.
Couples in from the cinema, during Intermission,
not wanting to let the story go, hugged it to themselves
like a scarf. I knew the men who'd go home to punish
their children and wives. I was faithful. Too often I refused
to provide an alibi for a man who only bought a half.
But sometimes I hestitated at a goodbye, wondered
how another man might seduce me. So when he died,
I bought the pub and closed it. The day I signed the contract
with the brewery (glad to be rid of a loss-maker on the moors)
I locked the doors, left what money remained in the till,
postcards from around the world, optics, beer mats, darts
in the board. Only the barrels and full bottles went.
Mornings I collect wood in my basket on wheels.
Coal, milk and groceries are left at the back door.
I could have been a woman who took the blame for men,
like Alice Molland, hanged at Heavitree. I share her name.

Visitors

Our night-time visitors leave clues. I hunt
them every morning, the way a park-keeper
might do the rounds. A brick knocked into plants,
the chicken wire of a fence folded over,
a lock jammed with wood to loosen a key.
I collect the unfamiliar cigarette ends, a bottle maybe,
newly broken twigs hanging from the hedge
and wonder how long they were here,
whether they used the swing, rope ladder
and trampoline, or just sat at our table
the way you'd stop outside a bar on a sunny day.
We never see them. Only the dogs know, barking
at 3 a.m., or cats, suddenly quiet in the middle of a fight.
They're in the company of hedgehogs, badgers, toads
and families of foxes. They've learned to be vigilant,
stay close to walls and away from light. At night,
different rules apply. Trees become human,
property's shared. They help themselves
to what's left outside, knowing if they make a mistake
the helicopter will be above them and men
with a night-vision camera will find their body heat
as noise fills the space between sky and earth,
and telephone lines wave in the downdraught.

Maradona, the Priest and the Jeweller

I've seen a woman watch me at the window
as I check stones for flaws, weigh gold.
I repair rings whose weakened claws
have shed diamonds into the sludge
of a U bend. Sometimes when she picks up
a ring, blushing, I see the deadly nightshade
among blackberries. Sweat appears
on her top lip as it will when she's soothing
her baby before the christening and its mouth
drags at her flesh. I understand why
she appears at the end of a runway,
or in a kitchen cupboard – her need
for a wishing tree draped with rags,
like my friend, the priest, who solved
the alchemy of Maradona's name
that summer as we argued his best moves.

Outside

A man's shouting "You whore, you fucking whore."
You open the curtain and the street light shines
a triangle on the mat. His voice is pulled up the hill
as if it's hanging onto a cable car all the way
to the hospital. He can think of nothing else –
a bass-line without the song. We hear her
once, quieter, "Stop it." He must have woken
the street. Friday night. She's too far away to grab
– backing down the hill, turning around to run
for a phone. Then the curfew returns – silence that waits
every morning for an opportunity, wills him
to wake up, wrapped around furniture, spinning
over demolition sites like a frisbee.

Blue Chevrolet

(for Jane and Erdam)

There are eleven of us in the blue Chevrolet Impala
as we bump to a garage to beg the loan of a jack.
The wheel nuts are solid. It takes three men to loosen them,
each stamping on the star shaped wrench until they give way.

One by one we fall into the shade while the men discuss
where to find parts, the money to be made hiring it for weddings,
with new lights and handles, a scratch along the driver's side
painted over, seats upholstered, clear of water bottles and sand.

I'd be married in this car, to the priest who called at 2 a.m.:
if I'd heard his name and remembered our meeting place –
the empty house with a butterfly on every stair, yellow and black
wings closed neatly as the letter I shouldn't have opened.

It's as wide as the road. We stretch our arms towards rocks
fluorescent with lichen, pine trees stunted at eye level
and fan wind in through the windows as the children on our laps
fall asleep – a head on each shoulder, folded into our bodies.

Opera plays in a beach cafe – the C of its name pronounced
as a ssh. A speed boat's moored at the jetty as if ready
for a getaway. And a man who could be a priest welcomes us.
He's carrying water, reminds me of a confessor.

There's absolution in this spectacle of island after island –
their shades of grey. And the blue Chevrolet waits under a fig tree
for the newly weds, ribbons hanging from its bumpers,
for a convoy of horns through hot streets with no passing places.

The Man who Speaks Four Languages

His voice is quiet, his accent's east-European.
He can't afford my grandfather's fees.
They talk in the waiting room, I listen
through a crack in the door. He waves
me in, finds a turquoise behind my ear,
a tourmaline in my dress pocket,
and rattles them together like dice
until they disappear. The next time
I see him, he's carrying a statue.
It's a boy, bending to pull a thorn
from his foot. The man tells me
how it reminds him of running
in woods without shoes, of his mother's
warnings. Now it pays for his teeth.
With it, he hands over too,
all those escape routes he planned,
nights with a knife under his mattress
calculating the depth of a fall, nights
wondering which furniture he could push
against a door, how much time he'd have
to grab the kids, whether he was strong
enough to carry them both, and how far?

The Major

(for Mrisi and Giya)

One day she'll explain why she's circling Dartmoor
driving north, west, south and east
through empty town centres, past Texaco's
rectangles of light. At Okehampton services,
a Starliner coach, windows blackened, is grounded
next to a diesel pump. She's searching for a phone
she can use without waking the children,
lifted away from a bonfire, where they lay
watching flames whiten a Tango can.
She follows signs for Launceston, turns
towards Tavistock. The major refuses to see
his sister, his nephew, his niece. He's forced them
to leave the party, summoned Whist Hounds
as she races towards Plymouth, sent mist
and driverless headlamps to blind her.
She ignores the map. Too late for a hotel,
she drives until the engine calms her,
towards a maze of single track lanes sunk into hedges.
A man breathing beer points to a field, warns
roads to the village close at 6 a.m. The major's command
cannot reach them here, will not stop the moon.
Mid-morning, its shadow arrives. She wraps the children
in a blanket. A rust-sailed barge lights its mast
as the sun's displaced. Later, on a beach of green slate
they celebrate. Her son brings mother of pearl,
her daughter a handful of white stones.

Lonely Hearts

By now he's cruising in the best
designer stuff – not flash, obscure; dressed
each night in labels worth a month's pay
from shoes to shirt in black and grey –
his shadow colours, shades of ink:
a walking ad, not that he'd think
of lonely hearts, or consider a woman
who'd answer one. Each night's on loan
and there's a library – leather bound, slim,
romantic, comic, porn and crime.
He can be anything or anyone he wants,
with no ties or history, he can reinvent
himself, read what they desire
quick as the fortune teller on Palace Pier.
He's their *I Ching*, astrologer or priest,
a witness, interpreter, rubber fetishist.
He's the freak preview of summer in March,
a child's first signature, victim-less crash,
the Saturday squandered trying on clothes,
Thornton's chocolates, an hour on the phone.
One gave him nationality, another a loan
for his sweat on their skin each morning.
His passport's never out of his pocket.
"Here's my name," he urges, "go on, check."

Cavern

Reggae, ska, soul and funk
US Garage, R&B

McCoy sharpens the handle of her steel comb
slides it into a thigh pocket.

Heavenly Jukebox, Felchley Hawkes
rockerbilly, 60's grooves.

Polly's slouched near an emergency exit
drinking McCoy's babycham and brandy.

Jerry Dammers, DJ Skitz
cheesey tunes and indy dance.

McCoy follows her friends, disappearing in twos
downstairs, through the door marked with a dress

Danny Rampling, Patrick Forge
jungle with an old school feel.

jabs the point against Polly's cheek
slashing it up to her only eye

tech house, hard-core, That's How It Is,
Jazz 2000, pop and trash

as £500 worth of foil glitters on the floor.
She's screaming, but the bass is too loud,

Big beat, blaxploitation, Latin
rare groove, Slinkey, Bullit, Breeze

grabs blindly at a sleeve, feeling sheepskin.
And McCoy, the girl she slagged off as nobody

reputable trance, hardstep, disco
Love Injection, Get It On

taunts her over the surf of the mix,
the refrains they both know by heart.

Meeting a Newsreader in the Lift

There is nothing but glass between me
and Birmingham's lights. I'm on the side
of the Hyatt, ears popping all the way
to a corridor where an empty
champagne bottle in a bucket, half-eaten
apple, and three glasses are marooned
outside room 2315; it's stuck shut;
aluminium windows, draughtproof
door, the bed slippery as satin.
I could be inside a carrier bag.
I have no compass and the only sound
is television. The lift stops for a newsreader.
Its silence and smoothness remind him
of cameras in a deserted studio
where he imagines thousands of people
in his invisible audience of millions,
making love – how he could interrupt
them with each headline.
At his floor, it's as if he's turned off.

Choir

Weekends and school holidays
I'd be up at five, catch the first
19 bus, walk the length
of Frensham pond to the kennels.
The barking began as I clanked
the gate. For seven hours
I'd be at their call until I knew
each one by voice: labrador, corgi,
dachshund, terrier, spaniel, setter
and underneath them all, the bass
tones of a pair of great Danes.
In music lessons, I heard nothing
else. I searched HMV and Virgin
for recordings, began taking
my mini-disc to work – trained
them with chocolate drops. I played
them Santana, John Lee Hooker,
Les Voix Bulgares, Sufi chants
and *Madame Butterfly*. I learned
what pitches they responded to.
Since then I've conducted choirs
of dogs worldwide: hyenas
in southern Africa, *chiens méchants*
throughout rural France, packs
of mongrels gone wild in Buenos Aires.
Dogs understand harmony – listen
to hounds mimic a hunting horn.
When I staged a concert inside
the Arctic Circle, it was minus 4.

As I struck my tuning fork,
the Northern Lights shuddered
and 900 huskies howled
from their cages. My next project's
soloists. I'm auditioning wolves.

Drought

"If I were called in
To construct a religion
I should make use of water."
Philip Larkin, 'Water'

She empties cupboards, stockpiled
with Perrier and Badoit, fills the bath.
Bubbles attach themselves to the hairs
on her skin like pike eggs and fizz.
On motorways criss-crossing Europe
and America, pantechnicons are hijacked
for their still or sparkling cargoes.
Water wardens patrol cities
to prevent cowboy plumbers
welding diversions from the mains.
Businesses advertise for diviners,
fly them over dusty plains. All they see
are uneven lines of bowls carried
by women or girls with perfect
deportment and dry eyes.

Escape Route

We arrive in the Anglia, legs prickling
with pins and needles, to gape at the turrets
of the Château du Lac which has no lake
but views of the Atlantic from the roof.
We want to find that tunnel; stamp
on leaf mould, press ears into moss
to listen; guessing it'll follow
a straight line through the woods
to an exit, blocked, grown over; a mouth
of stone bricks, each a foot thick,
collapsed rafters – mistaken over the years
for a mine shaft. There'll be steps up,
a stream running down, a plant straggling
out of a wall like cloth ripped on a nail
when a sailor's most accurate clock
was the moon, the sea's edge a fall into space.

The Time it Takes an Echo

At weekends the only rocks for miles
are crawling with climbers.
Their harnessed limbs
stretch over the dull strata
eroded into faces. A field away,
my children discover the echo.
Their voices hit the rocks like tennis balls –
higher notes bouncing back,
others continuing secretly
into the woods behind.
We wonder, 400 years after Mersenne,
how long it takes an echo to return.
The sounds travel past us,
across the railway line and the words,
although once theirs and mine,
become the property of air,
its humidity and wind.

Premonition

Before she gave birth
she dreamed of a litter of rabbits,
deformed puppy.

After, she watched her babies drown,
screamed their names uselessly in woods,
across motorways.

If she knew how to read them, she'd throw giblets
on an altar, slice open a goat – just to be sure.
The nightmares shame her.

She'd like to twist them into a wick,
surround them in wax,
let them burn slowly away.

Graveyard Jam

She's the dead princess but can't lie still
on her bed of stones, preferring to fill
the metal vase with them until Barbie
takes her place, her brother brings Aladdin,
and they become Batman and Robin, swooping
over this forgotten rectangle, falling off
its shattered kerb into grass
the strimmer's missed. I pick blackberries,
so huge they fall into my hands
as I try not to disturb webs knitted
over brambles like netting to discourage
birds. Woodlice drop off the fruit
into my plastic bowl, the sun is warm.
We stay among the old graves. There are
no paths into the tangles of thorns,
like on the racecourse or the Downs.
Maybe it's the thought of what feeds them,
just up from the catacombs, around
the mausolea cut into a bank topped
by trees, of how suckers envelop
crosses, headstones, angels and obelisks,
until there's no name, dates or tribute,
just jam in old jars of peanut butter, pesto
sauce, olives, pickles, stored in the dark
for winter breakfasts or sponge cakes.

Sketches of Women

It has to be murder – a woman's head
emerges from a vegetable patch, buried
in a Sainsbury's bag. They're fooled by the hair
and amount of flesh, but forensics discover
she's Victorian; traced to a crypt in Highgate.
He's charged with grave robbing. The magistrate
can't persuade him to plead as a man.
He wants to live as, and be called Karen
while he earns a prescription for hormones.
The skull was part of an earlier ritual,
when he straddled a white horse under a full
moon, then stood in its eye, turning three times
for luck. He was the rider it lost in centuries
of scouring from Bronze Age to Arthur and fairs
in the Vale. The long sweeping curve of its back,
a fertility totem – much more than a landmark.
Jumbled up with magic, acid and leylines
that summer on the hills s/he sees corn
ripple the way a wall melts in a hallucination
and envies the figures who run to the stones –
Snow White and the Dwarfs, Tom & Jerry,
Mickey Mouse – their primary colours, luminosity.
The morning of solstice there isn't a sun, just
dull grey and wet grass drenching his socks.
Later he vomits where he sits with friends in a circle
and over the music, half hears a girl
explain how the quality of what you get
is so random; how it's made pure, then cut.

Charon

All day long collecting pennies. I'm like a toilet attendant
underground at a station, damp walls, the constant smell.
Perhaps I should be painting eyelids instead
behind a curtain, smoothing cream over
grooved faces, placing slices of cucumber
neatly into sockets as if I was decorating
pâté. Five faces a morning, sable following
the bulge of the eyeball, dusting purple
into a network of lines, open pores. I wouldn't age.
I'd have my flesh sliced open, pulled back, stretched
as far as it would go over my ears.

I'm not just paid in pennies, though I had one
crusty with lava (a souvenir). He boasted of walking up
a volcano for it. Reminded me of the rush from Pompeii.
I've had plenty of shells, Egyptian bronze, brittle wooden planes.
Family porcelain is a favourite, they hand it over
still murmuring over the marks underneath.
It all goes in the chest. This padlock's ancient as stocks.
Now there are combinations, numbers instead of grooves,
rooms with magnetic key cards. But I love the click
as the key turns and the steel springs up –
each unlocking, an achievement.

That, and my pockets, are the only relief from the crying.
Then there's the splash of my oars. That gets them going
until they spot a man trying to put out a fire in the clearing
he's coppicing. It keeps erupting from beneath the forest floor;
he's miles from water, beating smouldering undergrowth,
and above him are the birds, wings in flames, spreading
it across fire-breaks as they plunge like rags tied to arrows.

Windmills

At the top of the hill, graves are marked
only by trees. You're buried in cardboard
without a name. It's full. The copse
will be the highest in the town.
Across the road we pant up towards
newer graves. Rows of metallic windmills,
the kind you can buy on the seafront,
spin in the wind. It takes a while to realise
this is where the white coffins are lifted
from lumbering hearses, shorter
than rabbit hutches, lighter than the flowers
shaped into favourite toys: babies who stop
moving in the womb; meningitis, cancer,
cot deaths, the two girls murdered in Wild
Park. Their stones are white marble
back rests for waterlogged teddy bears.
All the children are buried together –
like Jews and the rows of German soldiers
or those creating the copse, who prefer
to be anonymous, or the cremated,
among rose bushes and woodchips.
The rest are rediscovered people or the famous
whose front doors you could never have knocked on;
names taken from telephone directories and lists
of births, their dates arbitrary as lottery numbers.
They're kept away from us by a flint wall –
thousands of stones and for each, a body.

Party

[illegible]e room's filling up with people I've known.
[illegible]ey leave wine circles on the mantelpiece,
open windows, change tapes in the cassette,
flick through books and photo albums.
Someone's taken yesterday's paper from the bin
and is looking for a story. They tell each other
about themselves, kiss at the bottom of the stairs,
turn down lights and move into the garden with cushions
and rugs. They eat bite-sized tarts and tread on toys,
twist hair and press pendants into thumbs, scratch and cough.
Some have come back from the dead. They cling to drainpipes
and stand on shoulders, stretch for upstairs windows.
The hall is packed and cars fill the road, spill up side streets –
they've reached the racecourse. Floorboards give way,
collapse into the cellar. The music's so loud it interrupts
my heartbeat. My clothes are handed out to those who are cold.
All the paper in the house is torn up to write numbers on.
They take over the cemetery. A hotel pianist
and bass-player I fancied set up a stage with fallen
headstones. Friends with children organise a crèche.
A succession of plumbers who never understood my boiler
spot-weld standpipes. The detectives and para from Aldershot
who once lived upstairs, arrange a military display.
Part-time djs – van driver, computer salesman
and personal trainer from the gym – spin three decades,
45s to CDs. All the men I've ever been out with
are put in discussion groups by women friends.
Women from the ferries, shops, kennels, bars, temp agencies
and language school arrange shift work at minimal pay
for the handful of chief executives who've shown up. Relatives
have comfortable chairs away from the party
and all those cash-only landlords offer free rooms overnight.

Photographers take polaroids of everyone.
A man from the allotments hands out runner bean poles
and the electrician's run a cable to a photocopier.
Every face is enlarged to the size of a flag
as in demonstrations for the missing – husbands, wives,
toddlers, teenagers, street children, grandfathers,
aunts, cousins, neighbours, workmates, friends.

GAGARIN'S MOON

Gagarin's Moon

(Every month, the moon returns to the same place
in the sky as the day a child is born.)

Over the hoover, my mother sings 'Moon River',
or what she knows of it, "wider than a mile",
da daa dada da daaa, humming the rest
as she dresses naked dolls. The song's from
Breakfast at Tiffany's, Mercer and Mancini's
Oscar win of 1961. Just after midday, nearly full,
it's faded and blurred as a washed-out print.
But at night, my mother brings binoculars,
names craters and seas, lets me scan the surface.
It's as if I'm there, just looking over a hill.
I want to fill its holes with milk, hate
anyone giving it a face. The moon in the day
is a tunnel into these nights. The two of us
so close, the sky enormous, this other place.

Sunbeam Talbot

The Guardia Civil is out of the picture.
Against a tinted backdrop with relief
the heads of two flamenco dancers just touch.
An airbubble above them is all that allows
the water to move, glitter to float and fall.
They smile as if they are not gasping for it.
It came from a souvenir shop at the port
in Algeciras, before the 10 a.m. ferry to Tangiers.
Franco's armed police everywhere, the open-topped
Sunbeam Talbot lures children at every junction.
In my front room now, the three-balled pendulum
twists under the glass dome of that clock
from my aunt's flat. Once I believed it would never
stop, that it would keep perfect time
as if the dome protected it from lost minutes,
extra half hours – a metronome behind
her new high-heels hurrying along the quay.

Hem

The newest skirt is waiting to be taken up.
She measures the hem with a three-pronged
dressmaker's ruler, arthritic hands bent
over the slippery cloth, pins in her mouth
which she'll line up true to the pleats,
as slowly as she walks to the park,
me and the kids bullying her towards spring.
When I clear her wardrobe, the clocks
have changed. I take out the pins, counting
off days. With each one, the bench just inside the gates
inches closer until she's looking down the avenue
at the sea ironed out and ready for summer.

Blue Mountains

The weightlifter, greasy with sweat, lifts bells,
heavy enough to break bone, above his face.
He's flat on a bench, legs bent to the floor
while a boy counts seconds off a stopwatch.
Moving to a rod and pulley, he forces it down
to his waist in two grunts, back straightened
by leather and webbing, hands gripped
into fists within fingerless gloves, as his neck,
embroidered with tattoos, expands.
I face the mountains, a denser blue than veins,
and fill their squared off peaks with lines.
There's no view, or shelter behind rocks.
But 44 ahead of the yellow shirt, I see
a frozen lake. Slabs, uneven as broken paving stones,
jut from its surface, pile up by the waterfall.
I slide my feet into holes left in snow.
At the top there's a bog under a broken crust.
I can't read the map, paths are gone.
It could drain heat as fast as the March morning
my aunt fell. Heat carried on escaping
as a doctor ran a fingernail over the soles of her feet
and she shuddered. When the white-out obscures
my boots I take a gamble, talking loud,
until a green jacket emerges in front,
and a stream, which must lead to the village.
The mountains begin to reveal crevices again.

Amateur Mechanic

After crashing the spindly gyroscope with blades
like dragonfly wings, he begins mounting slides
of larvae, lichen and transparent insects, dyed
with Grenacher's Carmine. Then, inspired
by the cut away head he keeps to show
his patients how deep the root of a molar
grows into the jaw, he decides to build
his own x-ray machine; puts an ad
in the next Exchange and Mart for a nearly
new Crooke's tube and walks to Wembley
to buy wire for an induction coil.
He calculates a two inch spark would be ideal.

His plan's to study the skeletons of smaller birds.
Like men who jump off the end of piers
he longs to strap his arms to feathers
and, given the connection between hand
and wing, he'll ask his newest son in law
to be a guinea pig, assures him, "there's no danger."
He promises to show me the two rows
of carpal bones arranged in their shallow
socket at the end of the forearm
as if he's standing once again at the bottom
of a cliff at St David's, ready to risk
anything for the sight of rare eggs in a nest.

Spy Plane

My grandfather unlocks his model glider
from the display case it shares with two Airfix
fighter jets. He tries to explain about thermals
and planes which spied on the Germans,
silent except for the click of cameras
above occupied France. He shows us
how he's fitted struts to the body, stretched
skin over its skeleton for resistance.
In the back garden, we launch it across the lawn,
anticipate its escape over the tennis courts beyond.
But we haven't got his skill. It crashes
into the raspberry canes. We'd be better collecting
lost balls, lobbing them over the wall into unseen games
to interrupt a critical backhand or serve.
We listen for the thanks, grunts and numbers
we have started counting on our fingers, repeated
shouts of "love" we don't yet understand.

Wings

The love of flying came from his father
who never made a career of it
but knew enough to build a plane
in the garage – putting the wings on
at a local aerodrome.
Perhaps it was being born in a valley.
His children knew the makers' names
as well as nursery rhymes,
brought up on airshows and long absences:
Westland, Sikorsky, Bell, Lockheed,
Aerospatiale, Dornier, Marcel Dassault,
Cessna, British Aerospace.
At Farnborough, they saw the first Harrier
rise vertically, heard Concorde break
the sound barrier, ate ice-cream
unknowingly, with military buyers.
The air doesn't allow mistakes, he'd say.
For him, engines were the start of history.

Album

All the photos at the front are of planes:
the makes written underneath, in white ink,
as if they were friends.

Then young men beside cars they've never driven,
flat chests pushed out, hands resting
on drivers' doors, proprietorial.

The prints, three centimetres square, slip
in and out of focus: miniatures without
brush-strokes to define unlined faces

or the shadows age adds to a class reunion.
Ex-girlfriends, five pages in, are nothing
but a jagged list and flattened blobs of glue,

topped by shreds of light-sensitive paper.
They might have been swimming,
or smiling self-conscious on a rug by a river.

Wendy, Moira, Janet, Elizabeth, Win.
His mother's kept her face
but lost her name from every one.

Next to those of sisters, children, even
the dog, a spidery *ma* or *mum*'s
been scratched, on each page, almost to a hole.

View

My heels sink into the heaped sand,
as if I'm climbing a dune.
I look down into my father's grave.
The priest hands me a silver stick,
topped with a ball of holy water,
tells me to shake it three times
the way you'd dry off an umbrella.
My brothers wanted a view – we drove
to every cemetery within five miles
comparing the qualities of stone and marble
checking for graffiti and broken crosses
while he lay in a hospital fridge.
From here I can see over town, across
the railway line. Crooksbury,
with its single pine, Hankley, Frensham –
where we watched birds flocking
above the reeds the autumn of his divorce –
all the places he walked the dog
are behind me. I've been back once.
The headstone wasn't up yet,
just a number. I knelt only to plant bulbs
in a rabbit's abandoned attempt at a burrow.

Fire-eater

The summer roads to the twin ponds
buckle under flames ignited by a dog-end

I've already forgotten his name.
Fire-eater with the Cirque Bidon.

He took a Navajo silver cross
in return for my only bout of scabies.

But he could have pulled out clumps
of heather from those two commons, gulped

the flames the way he did me, until
we both had smoke in our nostrils.

Football

You suggest the Bar Italia, its oversized
TV screen hung from the ceiling
showing endless football. Impossible
to talk, I strain for sentences lost
in the milk froth of the coffee machine.
Chocolate powder sweetens the back
of my throat like phlegm.
There's nothing left to say.

Absent

Our neighbours' daughter calls her friends.
"They're out," I tell her, toys motionless,

cooker and TV off. I'm washing clothes, dishes,
sweeping the floor. I drink coffee until I feel sick.

Today they won't drop socks, spill apple juice
on the worktop; I'm listening to the news

as two magpies land on the wall, carry off
a burned-out nightlight, forgotten bangle.

From my Window

I watch my daughter swing
on a tyre until our apple tree shakes.

My son's picking lemon balm,
catching grasshoppers.

The cat's rolling in the flower-bed
among the hydrangea, hollyhocks,

feverfew my mother grew
from seed. And you're stretching

wet goatskin onto a drum.
I should be outside.

Peacock

Tonight you'll slide into bed again at 3 a.m.
the two children warm beside me, the red time
all I can see, a broken digital square, the dark
a withie bender criss-crossing above us, at its edges
the supple new shoots of a willow bent
towards a stream by birds: wren, thrush,
blackbird, starling, wood pigeon, finch.
Those branches are thin as the baby's arm
reaching out towards a needle which pierces
its amniotic sac, fingers stretched like ridges on a shell,
sensing only invasion, a movement in their warm
pool, my heart as I watch the point withdraw.

You enter this breathy darkness the way
a peacock stalks around us at the end of a picnic
walking on twigs without breaking them,
its tail catching on brambles, shedding
feathers dipped in turquoise and green.
The children feed it grapes, our only visitor for days,
mimicking its scream under dense pine trees
where we can't feel the sun. They call to it,
chase it through undergrowth and want peacocks
now on every walk, in every farm we pass.
And the feathers we bring home will float
on heat from the kitchen fire, rest under the table;
tokens of that uncompromising fan we waited for.

Golden Highway

i

We're too late for the whales; viewpoints
empty, telescopes abandoned. A month ago
the sea would have been bigger with them.
We stare, hopeful, at waves breaking over
a small island; willing it to move, to arch
its meaty back and slap its fins into the swell;
the way repeating a word somehow changes it.

I'm too cowardly to swim. The sea's chilled
with ice-floes. Your mother watches us walk
along the beach; we're the last to leave.
You lay down a bottle to collect a wave.
This is the end of a continent, jutting
into an evaporating ocean. Even you burn
under this sun. It reflects off white Mercedes
bumper to bumper on the Golden Highway.
It lifts the road feet off the ground
into a watery no-man's-land; scorches
streets which swallowed African names
to become Beaufort West, or Richmond.
It hammers through windscreens
as pantechnicons, travel north and south
with fruit, meat, wine, juice, cheese.

The Golden Highway squeezes sweat
from us across the Karroo. The baby cries for milk.
We stop in the shade to gulp warm water,
rinse hands and mouths.

ii

We leave Orange Farm, map reading badly
towards our road south, drive past the refinery
and smaller, growing squatter camps, whose zozos
turn rain into gravel on the roof at four
each afternoon. It's as if you're living inside a rattle.
Each drip trickles down the electric flex
to soak the mattress again. Away from
the houses, a cemetery's prepared for Christmas.
It has three rows of 20 trenches, red earth heaped
beside them like termite mounds.
Long-tailed black and red birds flap around like priests.
These are marshlands; even in high summer,
jumping clumps of reedy grass you slip
into unexpected springs. We're here to find
your brother's grave. Our son watches ants scuttle
underground as the sun climbs. Your mother,
anxious, paces unmarked paths between the rows
until she finds the white dome,
small china ornaments; his memorials.

iii

In the pool of our borrowed garden,
a young cobra's fished out, still alive.
In the house is a scorpion, suffocating in a jar.
Road signs are holed with bullets.
The people of the Karroo are lighter
but their bones don't change.
We recognise them from the museum.

We count ostriches and aloes for hundreds
of miles. When we can go no further
we see zebra. All you can say is:
Liberals love their black and white stripes.
I run as you splash water on my head
but I'm held back by milk fat, heavy breasts,
eyes always watching us. My feet sink
into burning sand, I wiggle my toes deeper.
You'll celebrate this first year
in exile, but at least it will be spring
and perhaps the arguments will end.

In Johannesburg, we buy cloth to take home,
beaded bracelets, skins, a woollen skirt,
dodging lethal taxis in streets
near the mirror-glass Stock Exchange.
Sitting in shade by a building site
is a man you grew up with in the countryside.
He's been waiting all day for work.
I meet more of your old friends.
They're like stones. I try to picture them again,
next to hanging nests of weaver birds,
a snake coiled under the front door,
your mother dancing on Christmas Day,
two circumcision processions,
the simplest words I failed to learn:
avhuxeni, ahee, minjani, nipfukile.

Walking

The man walking alone on the road
wrapped in a blanket, knows a lift will come.
A hundred miles between petrol stations
with his country beyond a range of mountains
to his east, he feels his muscles relax
as the gradient straightens out
after the long haul up from the wine region
with its vineyards, water tanks and grass
cooled by mist. Now there will be nothing
but lay-bys with trees and no taps. He carries
water, used to this trek, and knows someone
will stop. There's no need to put out a thumb
on a road like this, where crossroads are rare
as water, speed is constant as the scrub.
It won't be holiday-makers; they flap past,
windows dark as popstars', languid hands
dipped in air as if it was a private pool.
It won't be lorries; pummelling the road
like jack-hammers. It may be a mini-bus
full of Sowetans with a spare seat, leaving
for Johannesburg at dawn, after trading
factory bought china, hand-painted pots,
for unwanted clothes. The man walking alone
is tiny at first. We see him for miles, bobbing
in and out of the mirage like a seal we saw
swimming in the bay near Cape Town.
Its tail, ragged as seaweed, kept pace
as you jogged from the fish wholesalers
on the jetty to the beach carpark. Then he's in
the mirror, his face gone as if it was flashed on TV.
There'll be another, like the nought
on the mileometer which keeps coming round.

Desert

My bed is high and slopes so I hold the baby tight.
The sun is pulled down quick as a blind.
A scream wakes me – I lost my grip.
Shouting, I hear your mother whoop
as I rescue our daughter from the floor.
Suddenly we're all dancing in our underwear
and laughing more than at any time in this morose
country; laughing at your mother's noise,
at you trying to open the knife sticky with mango,
at the dense silence in the bungalow
forcing us into whispers. You were sure
someone had heard we were here,
was breaking in to chase us out. This town's near
neighbours are replicas of itself, filled with Boer
graveyards. An Afrikaaner tries to sell you a flag –
the old one – suggests we visit the dam.
It's as if they've drained the desert. This lake's incongruous
as the whitewashed holiday homes with grass
roofs and tiled bathrooms. It steals heat
from the sun, pushing up against a curved concrete
cliff, edged with healthy trees. There are no aloes;
desert plants, they won't rustle when the wind blows.

Lighthouse

The minibus engine is straining
up to the lighthouse. I lose count
of the steps on the last stretch.
Air seems thinner under this sky,
stretched over water. The nearest blinding
land-mass is shedding icebergs large as islands.
We follow the sun down to a beach.
Not the one the settlers came to,
the start of the great trek. This signpost's
for picnickers. We jump a shallow river
to track bird prints, signing thumbs up
to your mother fending baboons off our supper.
They lope away, tails in the air.
I should thank you for bringing me here,
but for weeks I've been suspended
in that moment after a row,
before the front door's slammed.
When they met us at the airport,
I'd lost my voice. I was unprepared
for the couple washing a Rottweiler
in a toddlers' paddling pool,
the Coon Carnival, the man shouting,
"Where did you find the white woman?"
The house sets us apart –
its high ceilings amplify us;
carry our whispers up to the gods.

Christmas

i

Plums and apples are gone now. Houses
flatten the old fruit farm, long and ranch-like,
Dutch Reform. At night, security lights flash
circles on lawns, outdoor stages for cats
breaking the beam. Dogs leap at fences,
rattling mesh the way their owners might shake
a pedigree. Gardeners move in slow motion,
avoiding sudden moves, as if they're pushing thighs
against water. Released from the snarls
the road home feels like a dance floor.

This is exile for city whites; sudden power cuts,
unaccustomed poisonous snakes, serum
in the fridge, farmers as comfortable with guns
as slitting the throat of a screaming pig.
They have slipped through the necklace of mines
around Johannesburg: uranium, gold, sulphur, clay,
silver, dolomite, coal, diamonds; swapping
once comfortable suburbs for poultry sheds.

The nearest town is sixties Afrikaaner style,
austere as a frontier post, without statues or gardens.
There's nowhere to hang around, just car parks
and warehouse shops, one bank, one chemist.
It's Christmas Eve and we're buying meat – steak, sausages,
chops – sold in brai packs, clear plastic bags.
They could be windows into a body.
There's no shop assistants
in funny hats just the heat, not enough shade,
queues at the butcher's and guards at the off-licence
stacked floor to ceiling with beer.

At the bank they ask where you got your pounds,
not believing your passport; its stamps from Denmark,
England, Ghana, Switzerland like pressed flowers
in an inherited book. It takes more than half an hour
to change money. You'd think they were giving it away,
each form handwritten, slow as a child,
large, round numbers pressed too hard into the paper.
She can't work out the passport number, I am itching
to argue, you restrain me, knowing better.

ii

We lie on the bed watching a game show –
applause and crackling interference –
sleep end to end like the wax family
in Johannesburg's Museum of Africa
past the reconstructed bushman,
recorded resistance speeches. We raid
our children's stockings for the neighbour's.
Your mother peels vegetables
from the 'Deliverance' market;
feathery carrots, cabbages – leaves chewed into lace.

Driving here, the clucks from the chicken
trussed in the back are all that interrupts
our silence. We must come before dark,
your mother commands. People will be drinking.
We're in time for the coalman. You hoist our son
into his horse-drawn cart, pay for the bags
the Aga will burn all day tomorrow, warming
the fermenting African beer, stewing meat, boiling rice
and pap. Electricity cables droop like washing lines

above us, criss-crossing into an unfinished net
above this city of ochre and tin.

In the morning the smoke rises vertically
as if it, too, is determined to escape. Your brothers
arrive, prompting the first muffled row
about who was buying drink. Children come early
to share the soap we brought your mother
then splash around the standpipe with our son.
Plates are filled, washed, filled again
and everyone dances. I cannot.
She insists I must be out again before dark.

Market

Women pad benches in threes
sliding beads on strands of wool
to stitch into skirts with black-edged lines
of Ndebele houses, arms striped
to their elbows in the colours of your mother's home
green walls, red earth and the butter yellow
of irises wet with afternoon rain.
Men, thinner, stay inside, smooth
edges off shallow rectangular bowls, scoop
circles from long spoons for serving maize,
scorch designs in soft wood, plane and paint
blanket chests for newly weds.
They stand in shavings deep as leaves,
dry as the muti herbs and ground roots
which hang beside goat skins
and curled kudu horns from the Karroo.
A woman passes, arms stretched
with bouquets in cellophane, catching
sunshine like windows – each flower
or leaf, a feature checked from the pavement,
reassurance that what we know, continues.

Tree

The sky's so low, no-one sees
children asleep in a tree
limbs wrapped around branches
backs bent into the trunk's wider divisions.
Each night there's a watch
(an older child who doesn't match
leaves against palms, veins
over lifelines) listening for adults,
who'd pull them down.
The stones are being washed
as they wake and make for the beach
where they'll trace the symmetry
of roots in a red and yellow cliff,
attempt a fire before sun
forces clouds away and brings boats
into the bay, people to wooden huts
where they'll live for a day.

How Can I Say I Hate your Country?

When wipers on the hire car
pack up during a 4 p.m. storm
on the flyover into Johannesburg,
we panic. Drenched in minutes,
we flag down a police car
from the hard shoulder. One glance,
and they've decided we can take
our chances. In Afrikaans they order us
to follow. We crawl down the slip road.
We're locked inside, the rain's relentless,
our children imprisoned in car seats.
A horn blasts, I scream and swerve
as their rear lights disappear
through a curtain of water.
My tongue's ulcerous for days.
I imagine Motsamai licking clean
the floor in John Forster Square.
But how can I say I hate your country?

FLIGHT PATHS

Flight Paths

Lower Bourne

We watch the foxes over the stream
in rough grass below the woods.
My mother calls from the sink
when they bring the cubs out.
At night we listen to the vixen scream.
So when the old man with Jack Russells lays traps
we force his metal jaws shut,
dig for a day with seaside spades
a pit deep enough to break his leg, push
sharpened stakes into sand, camouflaged
with dead leaves, a lattice-work of twigs.

It Started with Ringo

Someone hears he's at home
and we're like twitchers with news of a rare bird –
on bikes up and down the lane, ready
for the white Rolls, any movement of the gates.

We want to be seen, imagine him studying us
from windows poking above the walls.
A lonely star with only children for company.
He'll invite us in, "swim in my pool,

listen to music, chat with Paul, George
and John," who happen to be visiting.
It goes on from there; collecting addresses
the way we swapped autographs.

Hidden houses are worth more
than a signature marked on a wrist.
Houses can't be lost, washed off.
We want a hello to play back

big as a Western; settle for blackberries
from Clapton's hedge, the postman viewed
through parents' binoculars, an Instamatic
wound on, ready for Collins to appear.

In between we feed squirrels crusts
of peanut butter sandwiches, watch
jays fly screeching over tight fences
and claim for themselves the tops of trees.

Waiting for Something to Happen

When the peonies come out, hailstones
batter the fullest heads into mounds of petals
as if a group of women had stepped out
of identical dresses and walked away.
We lift bikes over stiles and pedal the river
bank for views into back gardens,
the dry smell of cow parsley and grasses
as familiar as the sun on skin,
to the rope swing where the river's shallow.

Beyond the moss under beech trees,
studded with last year's husks,
roads funnel heat between banked hedges
and perimeters of rhododendrons,
while we count magpies,

blow shrieks from couch grass and unpeel
poppy buds, the petals like unironed
silk, wrapped methodically
as parachutes, trying not to tear them.

Elstead

At Thursley Moat I listen for curlews
with Rod. We walk over the bog
on a wooden path. Beside an oily ditch,
a sundew; just denting the membrane
of water, a raft spider waiting
for skaters. We sit in the sun. This is as quiet
as Surrey gets. Could I map it?
Above, a helicopter, to the right,
a road. A cough, shoe scraping board,
lawn-mower, a dog barking,
a horse; all draw radials of sound.
I'm hiding again in bracken,
holding my breath, watching friends
tread past unaware. It's 24 years
since I heard no cars, no aircraft.

Hankley

At weekends, or when evenings last
my mother puts us in the old grey Rover
with the dog and drives to Hankley.

In the pond, by the car park, fishermen
hunch under umbrellas big as tents,
nets slouched in the shallows, and summon

pike strong enough to take a hand off.
The water never moves. This is the place
in the woods we walk away from.

The pond's too much like home.
On the common we struggle through sand
churned up by trucks. She warns us

to stay out of the heather, where lost flares
and cartridges hide, unexploded. We walk,
and talk more easily than in the house.

The sky opens us up and in summer
it's as if fire cracks in every stem of heather,
burns in the sun on our necks

the prickly heat reddening my mother's hands,
in clumps of beaters, stacked like paddles
waiting for canoes, and a river to carry them.

Then it's gone. Leaving patches of charcoal,
maps of new territories scored into purple;
landmarks which will last a year at most.

There were Daleks here. We know
there are targets where soldiers lie low
on their stomachs and wait, like the pike.

Shackleford

(for Rob Fairbanks)

Andrew has a map out. He's reading
off names: Nine Acre, Great Piece,
Thorn Bears, Bar Field, Middle Horse
Hatch, Stony Windsor. He can track
his family over this acreage
and beyond, precisely as the pedigree
of a bull. Fields of pasture are lumpy
with burrows, neatly sown crops
eaten ragged. Rabbits grey as molehills
flatten themselves into grass, hunted
by a man from Special Branch, his rifle
silenced to a thud. Above him, a cow's digging
a hole into red earth with her hooves.
Another's supervising a dozen calves
under trees, while their mothers eat.
Rooks raid pig feed. They know Andrew's car.
By the time he stops at the gate, the sky's full
– a gust of charred paper, cackling.

Between Maps

I watch from the woods as neighbours dismantle
walls, share timbers, stones, cows, sheep, goats.
In 16 years the village vanishes. You can trace
a star – pace each path, seven of them,
climb to the ridge, stop to stroke a dead elm,
stoop through willows along the dry stream,

or jump stepping stones, stumble through ruts
in the track south, smell elderflower in a hedge.
The last one brings you in from cowfields, directly west
– to crouch on grass where the centre was.

Gomshall

Cattle, a smudged mix of Belgian Blue and Friesian,
shuffle towards us on straw, shove heads through rails,
curious. They're eating oranges, barley brewers
have finished with, potato starch from Walkers crisps
– like bored teenagers whose only entertainment's
a bus shelter, Saturdays between McDonald's and Burger King.

Lucas farms alone, predicts it won't be long
before fields are monitored by satellite,
their 80 foot tramlines, tracked from space
and the places where charlock, cleavers, wild oats,
couch grass take hold on weakened soil,
reduce the yield, will be clear as the Great Wall.

Subterranea Britannica

(*for Malcolm Tadd*)

A rock thuds in the dust. Silent children listen
as its echo floods a wormery of cellars
stretched to meet the demand for hour-glasses.

It enters the shells of their ears, sweeps
over Grace's name carved in a wall
and the date next to it, 1644.

It passes a mock Tyrannosaurus Rex roaring
at pickaxe marks, expands at a rifle range,
ammunition store, bomb shelter, hospital.

It shakes 200 plates from a nuclear shelter,
finds its way upwards, to emerge
into a railway tunnel, sudden warmth, drizzle.

Outside, the echo approaches a pensioner
folding £10 into her purse, a bricklayer
stretching his arms for relief.

There's no going back. It searches out
anyone who'll hear – occupying the space
left by a phone that rings, then stops.

A287

"Are we still in England?" my four year old asks.
I thought this was the heart of it: four-wheel drives
and radio masts, neighbourhood watch, gates
from back gardens into woods, a stray azalea
among bilberries. People here need shade, complain
if trees are felled. They believe they are poor,
with boats beached in drives. I see men on donkeys
emerge from the M25. Women walk home
along the A287, nine Sainsbury's bags on their heads.

Frensham

From the ridge you can see two ponds,
twins but only in name. The little one's
hidden, occupied by moorhens;
in summer, boys who strip off
and wade across for a dare. My father walks
clockwise, close to the water, then back
onto sandy footpaths, hard and grey.
Eyes upwards, he watches a flock
circling the pond. Another airshow.
He's with them; sharing the instinct of flight
learned from decades building planes
but never understanding the need to leave.

Reigate

I drive under flight paths. They hum to me,
accompanied by twin motorways, the way
my seven year old fills his head with music
building Lego worlds. At first it's like the sea,
never loud enough to drown the bell sounds
of birds, a stone dropping. It nags of routes
to places I've forgotten or never found.

North Downs Way

The Child

When the kite jerks
I feel the wind, become sails
to be filled, a stolen hat. It ducks
towards woods thinned by gales.

I pump, give it more height
aiming for a spinning silver disc
so small it blinks, a satellite,
sun-trapped particle of dust.

Like waving to a train
until it disappears
I squint to find the line again
trace it from reel to atmosphere.

Parachute, triangle, chevron –
molecules scatter the blue –
Chinese bird, box, Action Man –
showing what air and light can do.

Chantries, Hogs Back, St Martha's,
Harebeating Brow, Arthur's Seat,
Farthing Common, Picketts Hole,
Aviary Wood, Gorse Tor, Flint. . . .

The Waitress

In my mind I'm back in the woods,
on Box Hill wearing unsuitable shoes,
stumbling over ruts in the path.
It's like a party here at weekends.

Let me lie down, feed me grapes,
sliced apple. This is where I'd build
a nest, weave branches into a hammock,
sit in the V of a trunk. A wood reminds me
of lovers, home, tables, chairs, coal, sea,
gunpowder, fire. It tells time in shadows,
rings, in fern, moss, toadstools, lichen.
It's a view beyond the kitchen window.
Birch, oak or beech – it's the tree
I'll remember even when it's gone.

Holly, Hanging Hill, White Down,
Nut Wood, Fabs, Newlands Corner,
Great Kings, Whistlers, Robins Grove,
Squintels, Skeats, Jacks Hut, Dencher. . . .

Postman

I spend the day anticipating its end
when I'll be running below the ridge.
The sky's red with dust, fields, too,
houses, berries – rosehip, holly, yew –

jumping from a stile I hit the ground
with a flame. Puttenham to Compton,
past Watts Chapel to Piccards Farm
I time myself until sweat

warms my face and back. I tick
off landmarks – Eggs for Sale,
a fence I snagged a jacket on.
My red shoes can't stop.

Hognore, May's, Sibton, Postling,
Titsey, Shootfield, Cannon, Syle,
Bedlam's Bank, Roughfield, Ash Platt,
Joelands, Bluebell, Devil's Hole. . . .

Pensioner

The dog loves it, the water's so slow
sometimes it doesn't appear to move;
collects dust and leaves for ducks
to make trails through. In summer, fish

throw themselves out of trees. It's brown
as a burned-out car. I can keep pace,
follow hidden perch and roach, stand
aside for dragonflies, fast as lycra-skinned

cyclists behind me without warning. I need
the sound of water, the way it dulls or amplifies.
Floods and the marks they leave
remind us a river does not always flow.

Winders, Gangers, Betsoms, Star,
Shore Hill, Harvel, Lone Barn Farm,
Saddle Knob, Swingfield, Coldblow,
Old Wives Lees, Frith, Giddy Horn. . . .

Lorry Driver

By Maidstone I'm nearly there.
To my left, in and out of view, a chalk scar
rail link – mud and tracks, drilling gear.
There's all nations on the inside lane,

a trail of trucks, Portuguese, Spanish, Italian,
one man operators, multinational logistics firms
soft sided, refrigerated, shuttling from
distribution centre to warehouse, back again.

My daughter's in Wye. When I walked on the ridge
a bonfire was dying in an empty field;
no sign of the motorway, just threads of smoke,
spires, knitted fields. At the Devil's Kneading Trough,

a boy with remote control plane swooped
it into the trench, for the thrill of the gradient.
The Channel was sharp in the distance.
I'd've jumped in the lorry to smell it,

listen to klaxons as ferries arrive and leave,
extractor fans droning from the tunnel,
to witness a continent pouring
into its neighbour, a shared sea parting.

Golden Hill, Crow Down, Cootings,
Charing, Haystack, Robin Hood,
Whinny Hill, Amber, Stowting,
Three Barrows Down, Partridge Wood. . . .

Teacher

Kids work better when it's sunny,
like cats and horses they're too wild
in wind. These day trips are a summer-term

treat; fields of rape flowers,
lazy picnics. Outside in the sun
it almost doesn't matter what they learn.

I'd trade this view if they remember,
there's no need to paint each stalk
of wheat or count each shade of yellow.

No Man's Acre, Chevening,
Wrangling Lane, Hart, Lenham Cross,
Plantagenet's Well, Snow Down,
Shakespeare Tunnel, Common Marsh. . . .

Data Miner

Mist sits in layers. Oast houses,
beamed roofs, point through, their shapes
only suggestions of what lies below.

People emerge from it, voices first,
step towards me, no warning.
Mist is a gift. All that matters

is putting one foot in front of another,
breathing, listening to stones.
Mist immerses you like a river from the sky.

It has no edges, beginning, end, top or bottom.
It sends light back to its source.
It holds all the names along the trail

Godmersham Park, the Stour, Chilham Castle,
the Tickled Trout, Boxley, St Martha's,
Coldrum Stones, the Wey – eight castles, churches,

farms, and wipes them out. All that matters
is putting one foot in front of another.
Concentrate on escaping. Take a whistle. Listen.

Moor Park, Caesar's Camp, Farnham,
Light Hill, Long Hill, Abbot's Cliff,
Horse Shoe, Bekesbourne, St Dunstan's,
Canterbury, Buckland, Dover.

Also published by Leviathan

Roger Finch

Fox in the Morning

ISBN 1-903563-05-4 (cased)
1-903563-06-2 (paperback)

Kit Wright

Hoping It Might Be So

ISBN 1-903563-00-3 (cased)
1-903563-01-1 (paperback)